Fun Fan Facts:
The Unofficial NBA Edition

Dallas Mavericks

Everything Young Dallas Mavericks Fans Should Know

By: Jake Liam

Dedication

To every Mavericks fan who woke up at midnight on February 2, 2025, saw a notification on their phone, and had to sit down on the bathroom floor for a minute.

You did not deserve that.

And to Cooper Flagg. No pressure, kid. We just traded the best player in franchise history, won the lottery at 1.8% odds, and handed you the whole thing.

Actually, yeah. No pressure.

Go Mavs.

THE NBA BY THE NUMBERS

MOST NBA CHAMPIONSHIPS[*]

CELTICS (18) [†]
LAKERS (17)
WARRIORS (7)
BULLS (6)
SPURS (5)

As of the 2024-25 Season. † One Trophy = 4 Championships.

BIG NUMBERS

$156 million
Stephen Curry's est. earnings in the 24-25 season

7'7"
Tallest player in NBA history (Gheorghe Mureşan & Manute Bol)

NBA HISTORY SNAPSHOT

1946 NBA Founded — **1954** Shot Clock Introduced — **1979** 3-Point Line Added — **2023** NBA Cup Introduced

30 | 4 | 82

30 Teams Competing in the NBA

4 Playoff Rounds

82 Games Per Season

DALLAS MAVERICKS
IN THE NBA

- FOUNDED: 1980[†]
- NBA TITLES: 1
- CONFERENCE TITLES: 3[*]

30 Playoff Appearances

*† Founding dates are complicated & may cause arguments at Thanksgiving. Ask someone born before color TV. All Titles reflect pre-relocation franchise history. * As of 2024-25 Season.*

EASTERN CONFERENCE

Atlantic – **Celtics**
Atlantic – **Nets**
Atlantic – **Knicks**
Atlantic – **76ers**
Atlantic – **Raptors**
Central – **Bulls**
Central – **Cavaliers**
Central – **Pistons**
Central – **Pacers**
Central – **Bucks**
Southeast – **Hawks**
Southeast – **Hornets**
Southeast – **Heat**
Southeast – **Magic**
Southeast – **Wizards**

WESTERN CONFERENCE

Pacific – **Lakers**
Pacific – **Clippers**
Pacific – **Warriors**
Pacific – **Suns**
Pacific – **Kings**
Northwest – **Nuggets**
Northwest – **Timberwolves**
Northwest – **Thunder**
Northwest – **Trail Blazers**
Northwest – **Jazz**
Southwest – **Mavericks**
Southwest – **Rockets**
Southwest – **Spurs**
Southwest – **Pelicans**
Southwest – **Grizzlies**

NBA ALL-TIME MVP LEADERS

KAREEM ABDUL-JABBAR (6) ★ MICHAEL JORDAN (5) ★ BILL RUSSELL (5)

Introduction

Welcome, fans! Whether you're new to cheering for the Dallas Mavericks or you've been bleeding the team colors your whole life, this book is packed with fun, exciting facts about your favorite team. Get ready to impress your friends and family with everything you know about the Dallas Mavericks.

Quick Time Out

This book is packed with stats. Like, A LOT of stats. Every fact was checked, double-checked, and triple-checked. But here's the thing about basketball history: not everyone agrees on everything. Ask someone who watched games before color TV and someone who grew up with instant replay and you'll get two completely different answers. My dad, stepdad, uncle, and grandpa all argued about the same fact. Four people. Four answers. All of them think they're right. So if you spot something that doesn't match what you've heard, congratulations. You might be a bigger fan than the people who helped make this book. And honestly? That's pretty cool.

HOW IT WORKS

THE SEASON
82 Games. One Goal.
Each team plays 82 games.
Win enough to make the
Playoffs.
Every game counts!
PLAYOFFS
30 Teams. 16 Make It.
8 per conference make the playoffs.
Win=Advance | Lose=Go Home
Best record
gets home court!
PLAYOFF ROUNDS
Best of 7. Win 4 or Go Home.
4 rounds of pure pressure.
Every series is do-or-die!
OVERTIME?
5 More Minutes.
Keep playing until
someone pulls ahead.
No ties. Ever.
THE FINALS
One Series. One Champion.
Winner lifts the Trophy.
Legend status unlocked.

How the NBA Works

At first glance, basketball feels simple. Ten players. One ball. Two hoops. Go.

Then the NBA adds the layers.

An 82-game regular season. A draft where bad teams pick first. Playoffs that last two full months. Superstars who can change everything with one trade. Dynasties that rise, fall, and rise again.

And somehow, it all works.

The NBA is built on one big idea: every team gets a chance to reset, reload, and rise again. No relegation. No dropping down to a lower league. Just basketball, every night, from October through June.

It is a league designed for drama, stars, and comebacks. And once you understand the flow, it is impossible to stop watching.

The League Setup

The NBA has 30 teams, spread across the United States and Canada. Those teams are split into two conferences:

- Eastern Conference
- Western Conference

Each conference has three divisions, mostly based on geography. Divisions matter for scheduling, but not as much as they used to.

Every team plays 82 regular season games, usually from October through April. Home games. Road games. Back-to-back nights. Long road trips. The season is a marathon before the sprint even starts.

Win games, and you climb the standings. Lose too many, and the pressure builds fast.

How Games Are Played

An NBA game has four quarters, each lasting 12 minutes. That means 48 minutes of game time, plus timeouts, free throws, and the occasional coach argument that adds another 20 minutes nobody planned for.

Scoring is simple:

- A shot inside the three-point line is worth 2 points
- A shot beyond the arc is worth 3 points
- Free throws are worth 1 point

If the score is tied at the end of regulation, the game goes to overtime, which lasts 5 minutes. Still tied? Another overtime. Keep going until someone wins.

There is a shot clock too. Teams have 24 seconds to take a shot. No standing around. No holding the ball forever. Keep it moving.

The Regular Season Race

The regular season is long for a reason. It tests everything.

Depth. Health. Focus. Patience.

Teams play opponents from both conferences, but they face conference rivals more often. By the end of the season, each conference's top teams have earned their playoff spots the hard way.

The goal is simple: make the playoffs. But there is a twist.

The NBA Cup

In 2023, the NBA added something new to the middle of the season. Something with actual stakes. They called it the In-Season Tournament, now known as the NBA Cup.

It works like this: Every team plays a small group stage during November and December, with special court designs that look like nothing else in basketball. The best teams advance to a knockout round held in Las Vegas.

The winners split a prize pool. Players earn bonus money. And for the first time, a team could lift a trophy before the playoffs even started.

Some fans are still warming up to it. Some players love it. But the moment a team starts treating it seriously and a crowd shows up buzzing in December, it feels like something.

Which, honestly, sounds about right.

The Play-In Tournament

Instead of sending the top eight teams from each conference straight to the playoffs, the NBA added something new. The Play-In Tournament.

Here is how it works:

- Teams ranked 1 through 6 in each conference are safe
- Teams ranked 7 through 10 fight for the final two playoff spots

The 7 and 8 seeds have an advantage. Win once and you are in. Lose and you still get one more shot. The 9 and 10 seeds have to win twice in a row just to earn a first-round matchup.

It turns the end of the season into a sprint. Every game suddenly matters more. Fans love it. Coaches age rapidly.

The NBA Playoffs

Once the playoffs begin, everything tightens.

Sixteen teams enter. Eight from each conference. Every round is a best-of-seven games series. That means the first team to win four games moves on:

- First Round
- Conference Semifinals
- Conference Finals
- NBA Finals

Home-court advantage matters. Crowds get louder. Rotations get shorter. Superstars play heavier minutes. One bad quarter can flip a series. One great performance can define a career.

By the time the NBA Finals arrive in June, only two teams are left. One from the East. One from the West.

Four wins away from a championship. Four wins away from history.

The NBA Draft: Hope Begins Here

Here is where the NBA gets clever. Every summer, new players enter the league through the NBA Draft. Teams take turns selecting college players, international stars, and teenagers straight out of high school.

The teams that finished with the worst records get the best odds to pick early through the Draft Lottery. It is not guaranteed, but it gives struggling franchises a real shot at changing their future with one pick.

That means one bad season does not doom you forever. It might actually change everything. Some franchises are rebuilt by a single draft night moment.

Hope shows up wearing a new jersey.

No Relegation. All Pressure.

Unlike many global sports leagues, NBA teams never drop down to a lower league. They always stay in the NBA.

That does not mean there is no pressure.

Fans remember losing seasons. Owners make changes. Coaches get replaced. Players get traded. Every year is a test of direction, patience, and belief.

Stars, Systems, and Showtime

The NBA is famous for its stars. But stars do not win alone.

Teams need chemistry. Coaches need systems. Role players need to deliver on the biggest stages. One injury. One hot streak. One trade deadline deal. Any of it can flip a season.

That balance between individual brilliance and team basketball is what makes the league special.

Fast breaks. Buzzer-beaters. Game 7s. And moments that get replayed forever. That is the NBA.

Once you get the flow, it is pure electricity.

Dallas Mavericks Facts

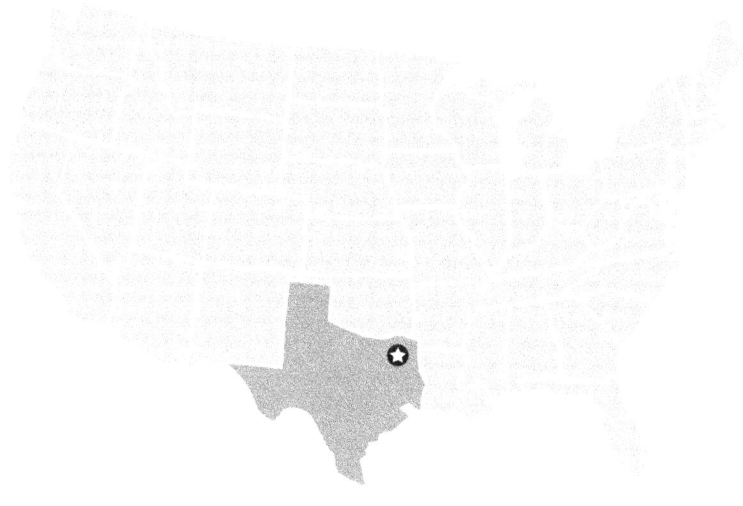

Home City

Dallas, Texas

Home City Metro Area Population

about 7.8 million

Home Arena

American Airlines Center

Max Capacity: 19,200

Famous Local Food

BBQ brisket, Tex-Mex, chicken-fried steak, kolaches

Conference / Division

Western / Southwest

Chapter 1: How the Mavs Were Born

1. A City That Almost Didn't Get a Team

In 1979, Dallas did not have an NBA team. It had the Cowboys. It had the Rangers. It had an enormous amount of Texas pride and an obsession with barbecue brisket. But professional basketball? Not their problem.

Then two guys named Don Carter and Norm Sonju decided to make it their problem. They marched up to the NBA and said they wanted an expansion team in Dallas. The league looked at them like they had asked for a third slice of someone else's birthday cake. There were already two NBA teams in Texas. The Houston Rockets. The San Antonio Spurs. The NBA was not exactly sitting around thinking, 'You know what Texas needs? More basketball.' They basically said no. Carter and Sonju came back. The NBA said no again. They came back again. Eventually the league got so tired of these two guys showing up that in April 1980, they just said fine. Take your team. Go away. Dallas had its franchise.

The city paid $12 million for the right to exist in the NBA. That sounds like a lot until you find out that someone later paid $285 million for the same team, and then someone after that paid $3.5 billion. Twelve million was basically the price of a nice parking lot. But the Mavericks were real. Whether they would be any good was a question nobody was ready to answer yet.

2. What's in a Name: The Maverick That Started It All

Before the first game was played, Dallas had to answer the most important question in sports: what do you call this thing?

The team held a naming contest open to fans. Thousands of suggestions poured in. The winner was 'Mavericks,' a word that comes from the actual history of Texas. Back in the 1800s, a rancher named Samuel Maverick refused to brand his cattle. Every cow wandering around on its own with no brand eventually got called a maverick. Basically: a rebel. Someone who does not follow the rules. Someone who does things their own way. The name also got a boost from a popular western TV show called Maverick that ran from 1957 to 1962, about a slick, free-thinking gambler who was always one step ahead of everyone else.

For a brand-new Texas basketball team trying to create an identity from scratch, the name was perfect.

Cowboys. Independence. Attitude. The logo had a cowboy silhouette. The colors were blue and green. The whole thing said we are not trying to be like anyone else. We are the Mavericks, and we do things our way. It is also just fun to say. Go ahead. Say 'Mavericks' out loud right now. It sounds like something a cowboy would growl before riding off into the sunset. The Rockets sounds fine. The Mavericks sounds like a movie trailer.

3. The First Good Years: A Run Nobody Saw Coming

New expansion teams are almost always terrible. That is not an opinion. That is basically a law of sports. You get handed a bunch of players nobody else wanted, you lose a lot of games, and everyone pats you on the head and says 'just be patient.' Most new franchises spend their first five years being very patient and very bad.

Dallas skipped most of that. By their fourth season the Mavericks had their first winning record and their first spot in the playoffs, powered by three homegrown stars: Mark Aguirre, Rolando Blackman, and Derek Harper. Those three were legitimate. Dallas made the playoffs five straight years from 1984 to 1988. They even made the Western Conference Finals in 1988, pushing all the way to the Conference Finals and one of the final four teams left in the entire league before losing to the Los Angeles Lakers. For a team that had not existed a decade earlier, this was remarkable. Mavericks fans looked at the future and felt great about it.

Then the wheels fell off completely. Core players got older. Trades went sideways. Draft picks did not pan out. The team that had looked so good at the end of the 1980s walked off a cliff in slow motion going into the 1990s. It is like getting an A on your first four tests and then somehow failing every single one after that. Nobody saw it coming, and nobody knew how to stop it. What happened next was going to be very, very ugly.

4. The Dark Ages: When 11 Wins Was Somehow the Answer

Okay. Brace yourself.

The Dallas Mavericks once won 11 games in an 82-game NBA season. Eleven. Not eleven in a row. Eleven total. Out of eighty-two. You have probably played a video game where you scored more points than that before dinner.

The early 1990s were historically, impressively, almost artistically bad for Dallas. In 1992-93, they went 11 and 71. The next season they managed 13 wins, which the team probably celebrated like a championship because it was an improvement. To give you a sense of scale: an NBA team plays 82 games. Losing 71 of them means you are losing about seven out of every eight games you play. If you were a Dallas fan driving to the arena in those years, you were not going to watch basketball. You were going to watch something that looked like basketball but ended in sadness.

The whole decade of the 1990s produced exactly zero playoff appearances for Dallas. Zero. For ten straight years, the Mavericks watched the postseason from their couches. The arena was half empty. The energy was somewhere between a waiting room and a sad aquarium. It looked like it might never get better. But somewhere in Germany, a skinny seven-foot teenager was quietly getting very, very good at basketball. More on that in Chapter 2.

5. Enter Mark Cuban: The Owner Who Argued With Everyone and Fixed Everything

On January 14, 2000, a tech billionaire named Mark Cuban bought the Dallas Mavericks for $285 million. He had made his money selling a company called Broadcast.com to Yahoo during the internet boom of the late 1990s. Before he owned the team, he was a regular season ticket holder who sat in the stands like everyone else. Then he bought the whole thing, moved four feet to the left, and sat courtside.

Cuban was not a quiet, suit-and-tie, stays-in-the-luxury-box kind of owner. He was the opposite of that. He showed up to every game. He screamed at referees. He argued calls from his courtside seat so loudly and so often that the NBA started fining him regularly. He paid the fines. Then he argued again. At one point his total fines added up to over a million dollars. He paid those too. Players noticed that this guy actually cared, like really cared, about winning, and the energy in the building changed almost immediately.

He also started spending money to make the team better. New practice facilities. Better travel. Bigger contracts. In Cuban's first full season in charge, the

Mavericks went from being one of the worst teams in basketball to winning 53 games and making the playoffs. Eleven wins to 53 wins in basically one year. The dark days were done. Dallas had its owner, it had its German superstar already on the roster, and a championship that nobody could see yet was quietly being built. The Mavericks were back. Loudly.

6. Rolando Blackman: The First Mavs Superstar (1981-1992)

Before there was Dirk, before there was Luka, before there was anyone worth buying a jersey for, there was Rolando Blackman. And if you have never heard of him, that is a problem we are about to fix right now.

Blackman was picked ninth overall in the 1981 draft, one year after the Mavericks became a team, which means Dallas got very lucky very fast. He was a 6-foot-6 shooting guard who could score from anywhere on the court, averaged 18 points a game over his career, and made four NBA All-Star teams. He became the first player born in Panama to ever play in the NBA. He also holds a Mavericks record that sounds made up but is completely real: in one game he made 22 free throws. Twenty-two. That is almost the number of free throws an entire team shoots in a normal game, and he did it himself, in one night, while the other team presumably stood there wondering what was happening.

For 11 seasons, Blackman was the face of the franchise. He played 865 games for Dallas and never once fouled out of a single one. Not one. In 865 games. He held the franchise scoring record for 18 years until a certain 7-foot German came along and took it from him in 2008. His number 22 jersey is retired and hanging in the rafters at American Airlines Center. Every great Mavericks team that ever followed owed a little something to the guy who showed up first and proved Dallas basketball was worth watching.

7. Steve Nash: The Point Guard Dallas Let Walk Right Out the Door (1998-2004)

This one is going to hurt a little. Stick with it.

Steve Nash arrived in Dallas in 1998, the same summer the Mavericks acquired Dirk Nowitzki, and the two immediately formed one of the most exciting partnerships in the league. For six seasons Nash ran the offense, racked up assists, made the All-Star team, and paired beautifully with Dirk to turn Dallas from a lottery team into a genuine contender. He was quick, creative, one of the best passers in the game, and everyone in Dallas assumed he would finish his career there. Then the summer of 2004 arrived. Nash was 30 years old. The team's doctors said his body might be breaking down. Mark Cuban offered him $51 million to stay. The

Phoenix Suns offered $65 million to come back. Nash took the bigger offer and left.

The next two seasons, Steve Nash won back-to-back NBA MVP awards. Two. In a row. Immediately after leaving Dallas. He turned the Phoenix Suns into the most exciting team in the league. He played another eight years of elite basketball. Cuban later called it the biggest mistake he ever made as the Mavericks' owner, which is really saying something because he made quite a few of them. The funniest part of the whole story is that Dirk Nowitzki, Nash's best friend and teammate, later said he actually encouraged Nash to take the Phoenix deal. So Dallas accidentally let one Hall-of-Famer leave, and the other one told him to go. It worked out fine in the end. But still. Ouch.

8. Dirk Nowitzki: The German Giant Who Changed Everything (1998-2019)

Imagine this. It is the night of the 1998 NBA Draft. The Milwaukee Bucks are about to select a 19-year-old from Wurzburg, Germany, named Dirk Nowitzki ninth overall. When his name is announced, the crowd in Vancouver boos. Boos. For one of the greatest players in NBA history. People at the draft actually booed this pick. Some of them have been thinking about that decision ever since.

The Mavericks traded for Nowitzki's rights on draft night, and what followed was one of the longest, most loyal, most decorated careers the NBA has ever seen. Dirk played 21 seasons in Dallas. All 21 with the same team. In a league where superstars get traded, demand out, chase other stars, and hop around chasing rings, Dirk stayed in Dallas for his entire career. He became the franchise's all-time leading scorer. He won the NBA MVP award in 2007. He invented a shot called the one-legged fadeaway that is nearly impossible to guard because defenders cannot tell if he is going left, right, or sideways through time. Coaches teach it now. They still have not figured out how to stop it.

The championship in 2011 was the peak of everything. More on that in Chapter 3. But the legacy is bigger than any single moment. Dirk Nowitzki is the greatest player in Dallas Mavericks history and one of the greatest players in NBA history, period. The guy the Vancouver crowd booed in 1998 ended up with his jersey retired, a statue outside the arena, and a name that every serious basketball fan knows by heart. The draft crowd was wrong. Very, very wrong.

Dirk Nowitzki stretches high for a soft one-handed layup while defenders watch and hope it misses. Good luck with that. Nowitzki spent his career lighting up scoreboards for the Dallas Mavericks, eventually leading them to the 2011 NBA Finals title. Seven feet tall. Jump shot like a guard. Not fair. Photo: Dirk Nowitzki vs the Washington Wizards. Photograph via Wikimedia Commons. Licensed under CC BY-SA 2.0. Source: Wikimedia Commons. *Photo: Dirk Nowitzki vs the Washington Wizards. Photograph via Wikimedia Commons. Licensed under CC BY-SA 2.0. Source: Wikimedia Commons.*

9. Jason Kidd: The Chess Master Who Was Older Than Everyone Thought (2008-2012)

By the time Jason Kidd arrived in Dallas in 2008, a lot of people thought his best days were behind him. He was 35 years old. His hair was going. His knees had taken a beating over a long NBA career with the Nets and the Suns. The general opinion around the league was that Kidd was a great player winding down, a name you added to a roster for leadership and experience and not much else.

Those people were completely wrong. Kidd took one look at the Mavericks, figured out exactly what they needed, and became the engine that made the whole machine run. He was not going to outscore anyone at 35. That was fine. What he could do was see the game three moves ahead of everyone on the floor. He knew where to be before the ball got there. He made Dirk's life easier just by being on the court. And in the 2011 NBA Finals, with the pressure at maximum and the whole thing on the line, Kidd was shooting threes in the fourth quarter like someone who had been doing it forever. He had. The Mavericks won the championship with an average team age that was politely described as 'veteran.' Jason Kidd was a huge reason why. Never count out the chess player who has been studying the board longer than everyone else.

10. Luka Doncic: The Kid Who Made Dallas Fall in Love All Over Again (2018-2025)

In Dirk Nowitzki's final NBA season, a 19-year-old from Slovenia named Luka Doncic showed up to replace him. Not intentionally. Nobody planned it that perfectly. It just happened that way, and the basketball universe apparently has a very good sense of drama.

Doncic had been playing professionally in Europe since he was 13 years old. By 16 he was starting for Real Madrid. By 18 he was the best player in European basketball. When he arrived in Dallas in 2018, he won Rookie of the Year. Then he got better. And better. And better. He led the NBA in scoring in 2024. He took the Mavericks to the Western Conference Finals in 2022 and to the NBA Finals in 2024. He set the franchise record for points in a single season. He recorded more triple-doubles than anyone in Mavericks history. Dallas fans watched him play and felt the same feeling they had felt watching Dirk in his prime, which is the rarest thing in sports: finding a player so good that you forget there has ever been anyone else.

Then, in February 2025, the Mavericks traded him to the Los Angeles Lakers. Without telling him first. He found out when the deal was already done. The whole city of Dallas reacted the same way you react when someone takes your last slice of pizza and then tries to explain it was actually a good decision. We will get into all of that in Chapter 5. But for now, just know that Luka Doncic gave Dallas something special. The city loved every minute of it. And the ending still does not feel real.

11. The 2006 Collapse: How to Lose a Championship You Already Had

Picture this. You are up two games to zero in the NBA Finals. You have the best record in the entire league. Your opponent is a Miami Heat team that barely made it through the East. Everyone on the planet thinks you are about to win your first championship. You are so close you have practically already ordered the trophy.

Then Dwyane Wade shows up to work.

In Game 3, Wade scored 42 points and dragged Miami back from 13 points down to win. In Game 4, he scored 36 and Dallas scored only 7 points in the entire fourth quarter. Seven. You can score seven points in a game of HORSE in your driveway. In Game 5, Wade scored 43 points and made 21 free throws in one night, an NBA Finals record that still stands. The Mavericks lost four straight games after leading 2-0, handing Miami the championship. Mark Cuban was so upset he was fined $250,000 for his behavior on the sideline. Dirk Nowitzki missed a free throw to tie the game in the final seconds of Game 3. He was so emotional after losing Game 6 that he walked off the court before the trophy ceremony was done and had to be brought back out.

The whole thing felt like a nightmare you cannot wake up from. But here is the thing about nightmares: sometimes they give you exactly the motivation you need. Dallas would meet Miami again. And the Mavericks were going to remember every single second of how this one felt.

12. The 2011 Championship: The Greatest Revenge Tour in NBA History

Five years after the 2006 disaster, the NBA looked at the playoff bracket and basically typed up a movie script. Dallas Mavericks versus Miami Heat. NBA Finals. Again. Except now Miami had added LeBron James and Chris Bosh to go along with Dwyane Wade. The whole league called them a superteam. They held a television special where all three of them stood on a stage together and promised each other championships. The phrase 'not one, not two, not three' entered the public consciousness and annoyed almost everyone who was not a Heat fan.

The Mavericks were underdogs. They had a 32-year-old Dirk, a 37-year-old Jason Kidd, and a bunch of veterans most people had quietly stopped expecting to win anything. Dallas went down 2 to 1 in the series. Then they won three straight. Dirk averaged 26 points and nearly 10 rebounds per game in the series while playing through a torn tendon in his finger. He scored or assisted on huge plays in the final minutes of multiple games. In Game 6, Dallas won 105 to 95 and captured the franchise's first championship. Dirk went to the locker room immediately after the final buzzer, sat quietly alone for a few minutes, and cried. The guy who had been called soft, the guy who had lost the 2006 Finals, the guy who had been doubted his whole career, had just beaten the biggest superteam the NBA had ever seen. The scoreboard does not lie. The Mavericks were champions. And it felt absolutely perfect.

13. The Dirk Fadeaway: A Shot That Should Not Be Legal

There is a reason the NBA has never figured out how to stop Dirk Nowitzki's signature move. It is because the move itself is designed to make defending it completely impossible.

Here is how it works. Dirk catches the ball, usually somewhere on the wing or in the mid-post. He faces his defender. Then he rises up and fades backward at an angle while releasing the ball off the glass or into the net with one leg kicked out for balance. The defender has two options. Jump with him and get your hand nowhere near the ball because Dirk is going backward and the angle is all wrong. Or stay on the ground and watch a nearly seven-foot man with a silky jumper score while standing over you. Neither option is good. Coaches have tried to game-plan against it for two decades. None of them cracked it.

What makes it even more unfair is that Dirk shot it off one leg, which sounds like it should reduce accuracy. It does not. He made that shot at the highest levels in the most pressure-filled moments of his career. He hit it on bad knees. He hit it sick. He hit it with a torn finger. When he was asked why he started shooting it that way, he basically said it just worked, which is the most maddening answer possible. Other players have tried to copy it. None of them do it like he did. Some shots belong to the player who invented them. The Dirk fadeaway is one of those shots, and it is never coming back now that he is retired. Enjoy the footage. It is genuinely worth watching.

14. The 2022 Suns Obliteration: A Game 7 for the Ages

Going into the 2022 playoffs, the Phoenix Suns were supposed to win the whole thing. They finished with the best record in basketball. They had Devin Booker. They had Chris Paul. They had knocked out the defending champions the year before. Everyone agreed that if you were picking a team to win the West, Phoenix was your answer. Nobody put Dallas on that list.

The Mavericks were down 2 to 0 in the series. Luka had put up 45 points in Game 1 and still lost, because no one else on the team scored more than 15. Then Dallas came back. They won four of the next five games to force Game 7 in Phoenix. And then Game 7 happened, and it was so one-sided it barely seemed real. Dallas won 123 to 90. On the road. In a Game 7. Against the best team in the NBA. Luka scored 35 points in just 30 minutes and did not even need to play the whole game because it was over so early. The Suns scored only 27 points in the entire first half. Luka scored 27 points in the first half by himself. Chris Paul, one of the greatest point guards ever, was held scoreless in the first half and finished with 10 points total. One of the largest road wins in a Game 7 in modern NBA history. Dallas fans had been saying Luka was special for years. After that night, nobody needed convincing anymore.

15. The 2024 NBA Finals: Dallas's Third Trip to the Mountaintop

Nobody predicted the 2024 Dallas Mavericks would make the NBA Finals. They were not the best team in the West. They were not even supposed to make it past the second round. But Luka Doncic and Kyrie Irving locked in during the playoffs and became the most dangerous offensive duo in basketball for about two months.

Dallas knocked out the Los Angeles Clippers, the Oklahoma City Thunder, and then the Minnesota Timberwolves in five games to reach the Finals for the first time since 2011. Luka averaged 32.4 points per game against Minnesota, was named the series MVP, and played like a man who had been waiting his whole life for that stage. The opponent in the Finals was the Boston Celtics, who had one of the most complete rosters in recent memory. Dallas won Game 1 and made things interesting, but Boston pulled away and won the series in five games. The Celtics were simply better. It hurt. But here is what mattered: the

Mavericks had done it again. A franchise that had been written off after the Dirk era, that had spent years rebuilding, that had handed the reins to a 19-year-old Slovenian and crossed its fingers, had made it all the way back to the Finals. Third time in franchise history. It would not be the last. And then, six months later, they traded the guy who got them there. But that story is in Chapter 5, and you are not ready for it yet.

16. Meet Champ: A Horse Who Has No Business Being This Charming

The Dallas Mavericks' mascot is a horse. A big, blue, fluffy horse named Champ who wears a basketball jersey and has a white mane and tail and the energy of someone who drank four energy drinks before the opening tip. He runs around the arena, high-fives strangers, sneaks up on opposing players' benches, and causes general joyful chaos every single game night.

Now. A quick vocabulary reminder. The word 'maverick' comes from a Texas rancher who refused to brand his cattle. A maverick is technically an unbranded calf. A calf. Not a horse. Champ is a horse. So Dallas named their team after a cow situation, and then the mascot they chose was a completely different animal. This is the kind of decision that makes total sense if you just go with it and stop asking questions, which is exactly what everyone in Dallas has done for decades. Champ even helped hold the Larry O'Brien Championship Trophy during the 2011 title celebration, which is a sentence that sounds made up but is completely real. A horse in a basketball jersey hoisted the NBA championship trophy. And honestly? He earned it.

The guy who created Champ, Jeff Goodin, originally played the team's other mascot, MavsMan, a human-basketball hybrid in a Spiderman-style orange suit who also appears at games. So the Dallas Mavericks have two mascots. One is a horse. One is a man who appears to be merging with a basketball. Between those two and Mark Cuban sitting courtside in a team hoodie, game nights in Dallas have never exactly been boring.

17. Two Arenas, One Franchise, and a Roof That Leaks

For the first 21 years of their existence, the Dallas Mavericks played at Reunion Arena, a building that opened in 1980, cost $27 million to build, and apparently had noise levels that reached 112 decibels in the mid-1980s when the crowd got going. For reference, 112 decibels is roughly the sound of a chainsaw. Dallas fans are not quiet people.

Reunion Arena was eventually torn down in 2009. In its place, the Mavericks moved to the American Airlines Center in 2001, a $420 million arena in the Victory Park neighborhood of downtown Dallas that they share with the NHL's Dallas Stars. The building has 19,200 seats, a giant statue of Dirk Nowitzki shooting his one-legged fadeaway outside the front entrance, and a street out front that was officially renamed Nowitzki Way in 2019. The arena also goes by the nickname 'The Hangar,' which is fitting because the arched roof and exposed steel girders make the inside look like the world's most expensive airport terminal.

One fun bonus fact about the American Airlines Center: in early 2022, during a Mavericks game and then again during a playoff game against Golden State, the roof sprung a leak. At the American Airlines Center. A building that cost $420 million. It rained inside. Players were dodging puddles on a hardwood floor worth more than most people's houses. Dallas fixed it. But for a brief beautiful moment, the most expensive arena in the city had the same problem as your uncle's garage.

18. The Sellout Streak: 23 Years of Showing Up (And Then Suddenly Not)

Here is a wild streak of numbers. Starting on December 15, 2001, the Dallas Mavericks sold out every single home game at American Airlines Center. Every one. For 23 years. Through bad seasons and great seasons, through rebuilding years and championship years, through everything that happened in between, someone always filled every seat in that building. By 2019, they had sold out over 700 consecutive regular season games, which was one of the longest active sellout streaks in all of North American professional sports.

Then came the 2025-26 season. Luka Doncic had been traded. Anthony Davis was injured. Kyrie Irving tore his ACL. The general manager was fired. And on October 29, 2025, for the first time since December 2001, the Mavericks did not sell out their home arena. Twenty-three years and ten months of consecutive sellouts, gone. Some fans were mad at the front office. Some fans followed Luka to the Lakers. Some fans just needed a night off after all the drama. You can understand all of them. The streak ended the same way the Luka era ended: suddenly, without warning, and in a way nobody quite saw coming. The good news is that

Cooper Flagg is already bringing people back. The seats are filling up again. Dallas fans are stubborn like that.

19. Mark Cuban's Fines: One Man's War Against Referees Everywhere

Mark Cuban has been fined by the NBA more than $3 million dollars total for arguing with, criticizing, confronting, and generally making life difficult for referees and league officials. Three million dollars. That is not a typo. That is the price of multiple houses, paid voluntarily by a man who simply could not stop himself from telling referees they were wrong.

It started immediately. He got his first fine in November 2000, a modest $5,000 for criticizing a referee. He then picked up two more in the same eight-day stretch, because once Mark Cuban starts arguing, he does not stop mid-argument. Then they kept coming. He once ordered arena employees to freeze a frame on the Jumbotron to show photographers a missed call. He walked onto the court during a game to argue a call in the playoffs and got fined $100,000. He screamed at the NBA commissioner during the 2006 Finals and got fined $250,000 for 'several acts of misconduct.' He wrote a blog post called 'How to Improve NBA Playoff

Officiating' and got fined another $100,000 just for publishing it. The single biggest one was $500,000 for a postgame Twitter meltdown after a loss to Atlanta.

To his credit, Cuban reportedly matched every fine dollar-for-dollar with a charitable donation, which means his running argument with NBA referees accidentally generated millions of dollars for good causes. There is probably a lesson in there somewhere about how even the most chaotic energy can accidentally produce good results. Or maybe the lesson is just: do not argue with referees. Either way, Mavericks fans loved every single second of it.

20. Everything You Never Knew You Needed to Know About Texas

For a state that has produced three NBA teams, Friday Night Lights, breakfast tacos, and at least four different opinions about the proper way to make chili, 'maverick' fits Texas pretty perfectly.

Dallas itself sits in the middle of one of the fastest-growing metro areas in the entire United States, with nearly 8 million people spread across the Dallas-Fort Worth Metroplex. The city is known for the Cowboys, for Texas BBQ brisket so good people drive three hours for it, for extremely hot summers that make outdoor basketball impractical from May through September, and for the kind of sports loyalty that generates 700-game sellout streaks even during years when the team is not very good. Texas also has a law that says you can own up to six cows, fourteen chickens, and one wild hog in the city limits of certain municipalities, which has absolutely nothing to do with basketball but is the kind of detail that makes Texas genuinely interesting. The Mavericks fit right in. Independent. A little unpredictable. Very, very Texan.

21. The Trade That Broke Dallas's Brain

At midnight on February 2, 2025, most of Dallas was asleep. Then their phones started going off.

Luka Doncic, the 25-year-old franchise cornerstone, the guy who had just taken the team to the NBA Finals eight months earlier, the player every single Mavericks fan assumed would be in Dallas until he retired, had been traded to the Los Angeles Lakers. For Anthony Davis. In the middle of the night. Without telling Luka first. He found out when it was already done. The general manager's explanation for the whole thing was, and this is a real quote from a real human adult who made this real decision: 'I believe that defense wins championships.'

Dallas fans reacted the way you would react if someone snuck into your house at midnight and replaced your dog with a different dog and then left a note saying the new dog plays better defense. People gathered outside American Airlines Center to protest. Someone started 'Fire Nico' chants at a Medieval Times dinner show. An actual medieval jousting restaurant. People were so upset about a basketball trade that they went to a place where knights fight on horses and started chanting about the general manager. That is a level of upset that does not have a name yet. The whole city was in shock. And things were about to get much, much worse.

22. The Season Where Absolutely Everything Went Wrong

Okay. Take a deep breath. We are going to go through what happened to the Dallas Mavericks after the Luka trade, and you are going to need to be sitting down for this.

Anthony Davis, the player they got back, played one game and got injured. Kyrie Irving, the other star, also got injured and missed the rest of the season. The general manager was fired in November. Davis was traded away again after playing only 29 games for a team that went 16 and 13 with him. Dallas missed the playoffs. The new ownership raised ticket prices anyway, citing 'ongoing investments in the team,' which is the sports equivalent of a restaurant burning down your meal and then charging extra for the smoke. Luka, meanwhile, scored 45 points against his old team the first time he came back to Dallas, cried before the game, then won by 15 while the city of Dallas watched from home.

At one point, a Dallas player named PJ Washington had to stop mid-free throw to yell at the fans that he was tired of hearing 'Fire Nico' while he was trying to shoot. The fans were chanting about the fired general manager during a live game. The man was already fired. He was gone. They were still chanting. It was a very long season in Dallas. But here is the thing about very long seasons: sometimes they end with a really, really good draft pick.

23. The 1.8% Miracle: When the Basketball Gods Felt Bad

The NBA Draft Lottery is an annual event where the worst teams in the league get a chance to win the best pick. The worse your season, the better your odds. Dallas had a 1.8% chance of winning the first overall pick. One point eight percent. If you flipped a coin 55 times in a row and it landed heads every single time, you would have roughly the same odds as the Mavericks had of winning that lottery. It is not something you plan for. It is not something you expect. It is barely something you hope for.

They won it.

Rolando Blackman, the legendary Mavericks shooting guard from the 1980s who you read about in Chapter 2, was the team's representative at the lottery in Chicago. When the first pick was announced as Dallas, Blackman sat there in a blue suit looking like a man who had been struck by lightning in the most wonderful possible way. Back in Dallas, fans lost their minds. A city that had been through the Luka trade, the Davis injury, the Kyrie ACL, the GM firing, and the ticket price increase suddenly had the number one pick in a draft that featured a generational prospect. The basketball universe had looked at what Dallas went through and said: okay, fine, here you go. One 19-year-old from Maine who might save your entire franchise. You have earned it. Now please stop chanting at the jousting restaurant.

24. Cooper Flagg: The Kid from Nowhere Who Is Going Everywhere

Cooper Flagg grew up in Newport, Maine. Newport, Maine has about 3,000 people in it. It is a small town where everybody knows everybody, the winters are brutal, and the nearest NBA arena is roughly six hours away. Flagg started playing basketball there, led his tiny high school to a state championship as a freshman, and was so obviously gifted that the entire state of Maine threw him a parade. He was 15 years old and the state of Maine threw him a parade.

He transferred to a powerhouse prep school in Florida, dominated there too, went to Duke for one year, scored 42 points in a single college game while breaking Duke and ACC freshman records, led the Blue Devils to the Final Four, won national college player of the year, and then walked into the 2025 NBA Draft as the consensus number one pick. The Mavericks selected him first overall and handed the keys of a franchise to a 19-year-old from a town of 3,000 people. He responded by averaging nearly 20 points, almost 7 rebounds, and over 4 assists per game as a rookie. He is 6 feet 9 inches tall, plays defense like it is personal, and has the kind of basketball IQ that makes coaches stop practice just to watch him figure things out. Bam Adebayo, a star center for the Miami Heat, watched Flagg demand the ball in the final two minutes of a close game on the road and said out loud: he is not scared of the moment. From Newport, Maine to the NBA. From 3,000 people watching to millions. The kid is just getting started.

25. Blue and Silver Forever: Dallas Is Not Done Yet

Here is where the Mavericks are right now. Kyrie Irving is recovering from his ACL tear and will be back. Cooper Flagg is already one of the best rookies in the league and is going to get better every single year. The team won the draft lottery against 54 to 1 odds and is building something new from the ground up. The sellout streak ended, but seats are already filling back up because Flagg is appointment television and Dallas fans are not the type to stay away for long.

Is it a little painful right now? Yes. Is the Luka trade still a topic of conversation that makes grown adults in Dallas need to sit down for a minute? Also yes. But here is what 45 years of Mavericks history teaches you. This franchise has gone from 11 wins to a championship. They went from a decade without a playoff appearance to Dirk Nowitzki raising a trophy over his head. They went from a 1.8% chance at the lottery to Cooper Flagg wearing number 32 and posting 27 point, 10 rebound, 10 assist games like it is nothing. Dallas has always found a way. The dark years never last. The championships feel twice as sweet because of them. The Flagg era is just beginning, and if history means anything in this city, the best is still ahead. Blue and silver forever. Go Mavs.

You think you are a true Dallas Mavericks fan? Try this bonus quiz!

1. The Dallas Mavericks joined the NBA in what year?

A) 1976
B) 1978
C) 1980
D) 1982

2. The name 'Mavericks' was inspired by a word that originally referred to what?

A) A wild stallion that could not be tamed
B) An unbranded calf owned by Texas rancher Samuel Maverick
C) A character from a famous John Wayne movie
D) A type of cattle brand used in the 1800s

3. Mark Cuban bought the Dallas Mavericks in the year 2000 for how much money?

A) $85 million
B) $185 million
C) $285 million
D) $385 million

4. Rolando Blackman holds a Mavericks record that sounds almost impossible. What is it?

A) Most points in a single game
B) Most three-pointers in a single season
C) Most free throws made in a single game with 22
D) Most consecutive games without a foul out

5. When Steve Nash left Dallas for Phoenix in 2004, what did he do immediately after leaving?

A) Retired within two seasons due to injuries
B) Won back-to-back NBA MVP awards
C) Led the Suns to an NBA championship
D) Was traded to the Lakers the following year

6. Dirk Nowitzki was booed at the 1998 NBA Draft when his name was announced. Where was the draft held that year?

A) New York City
B) Los Angeles
C) Vancouver
D) Toronto

7. In the 2006 NBA Finals, Dallas led Miami two games to zero and then lost four straight. Which Heat player put up 42, 36, and 43 points in Games 3, 4, and 5?

A) LeBron James

B) Shaquille O'Neal

C) Chris Bosh

D) Dwyane Wade

8. In the 2011 NBA Finals, the Mavericks beat the Miami Heat as underdogs. How many points did Dirk Nowitzki average in that series?

A) 18.5 points per game

B) 22.0 points per game

C) 26.0 points per game

D) 30.5 points per game

9. In Game 7 of the 2022 Western Conference Semifinals, Dallas demolished the top-seeded Phoenix Suns by how many points?

A) 11 points

B) 19 points

C) 27 points

D) 33 points

10. The Dallas Mavericks' mascot Champ is what kind of animal?

A) A longhorn bull
B) A blue horse
C) A coyote
D) An armadillo

11. The Mavericks' famous sellout streak at American Airlines Center began in December 2001. Roughly how long did it last before ending in 2025?

A) 10 years
B) 16 years
C) 20 years
D) 23 years

12. Luka Doncic was traded to the Los Angeles Lakers in February 2025 in exchange for which player?

A) LeBron James
B) Anthony Davis
C) Russell Westbrook
D) Kevin Durant

13. What were the Dallas Mavericks' odds of winning the 2025 NBA Draft Lottery, which they won to select Cooper Flagg?

A) 1.8%

B) 8.5%

C) 14.0%

D) 22.3%

14. Cooper Flagg grew up in a small town of about 3,000 people in which US state?

A) Vermont

B) New Hampshire

C) Maine

D) Montana

15. Mark Cuban was fined more than how much money total by the NBA during his time as Mavericks owner for arguing about officiating?

A) $500,000

B) $1 million

C) $3 million

D) $10 million

Super Fan Secret Challenge

Only a true Dallas Mavericks fan will know this.

(No Answer Provided)

Rolando Blackman represented the Mavericks at the 2025 NBA Draft Lottery. Dallas won the first overall pick despite having only a 1.8% chance. Who did they select with that pick?

A) Ace Flagg
B) Dylan Harper
C) Cooper Flagg
D) VJ Edgecombe

Answer Key

1. C) 1980

2. B) An unbranded calf owned by Texas rancher Samuel Maverick

3. C) $285 million

4. C) Most free throws made in a single game with 22

5. B) Won back-to-back NBA MVP awards

6. C) Vancouver

7. D) Dwyane Wade

8. C) 26.0 points per game

9. D) 33 points

10. B) A blue horse

11. D) 23 years

12. B) Anthony Davis

13. A) 1.8%

14. C) Maine

15. C) $3 million

NBA PLAYOFF BRACKET

* Fill in your picks and try not to argue with your friends about it!

Part of the Fun Fan Facts: The Unofficial Sports Guide Series

Be the Boss of the Playoffs

You've broken down the matchups. You know which superstar takes over in the fourth quarter. You've seen the bench units that quietly decide series. You've watched the adjustments coaches make when their backs are against the wall.

Now it's time to stop watching and start deciding.

On this page, you are not just a fan. You are the Head Coach drawing up the last play with three seconds left on the clock. You are the GM who built this roster. You are the analyst who saw it all coming.

This is not just filling out a bracket.

This is building your championship run.

Sixteen teams enter the NBA Playoffs. The path is brutal. Best of seven. No shortcuts. No hiding. Every round gets louder, harder, and more personal.

This bracket is your Playoff Control Room.

The Game Plan

1. Survive Round One: Start with the opening round. Which matchup is going seven games? Who has the closer? Who folds under pressure? Make the calls.

2. Feel the Momentum: As you move into the Conference Semifinals and Conference Finals, things change. Role players become heroes. Stars feel the weight. Trust your reads.

3. Own the Finals: Trace your picks all the way to the NBA Finals. When the confetti falls and the trophy is raised, you'll find out who earned it.

House Rules: Circle your boldest upset. That is your official "I knew it" moment.

Choose Your Weapon: Pencil if you want flexibility. Pen if you trust your instincts. Sharpie if you believe in chaos.

Because once the playoffs tip off, there is no rewinding Game 7.

Make your picks. Trust your basketball brain. And let the playoff drama begin.

Fun Facts Wrap-Up

You made it through! You're officially a true superfan! Now it's time to put your knowledge to the test. Share these facts with friends and see who really knows their team best.

Love the series?

Your reviews help other fans discover Fun Fan Facts. If you enjoyed this book, we'd really appreciate you sharing your thoughts and leaving a review.

Want more Fun Fan Facts?

Scan the QR code below to visit our site and explore bonus trivia, challenges, and special extras - including new teams, future series, and collectible fun as they're released.

Collect All the Fun Fan Facts Series!

Check off every book you read. See the full set on Amazon. Search "Fun Fan Facts Jake Liam."

World Cup 2026 Edition

☐ Algeria

☐ Argentina

☐ Australia

☐ Austria

☐ Belgium

☐ Brazil

☐ Canada

☐ Cape Verde

☐ Colombia

☐ Croatia

☐ Curaçao

☐ Ecuador

☐ Egypt

☐ England

☐ France

☐ Germany

☐ Ghana

☐ Haiti

☐ Iran

☐ Ivory Coast

☐ Japan

☐ Jordan

☐ Mexico

☐ Morocco

☐ Netherlands

☐ New Zealand

☐ Norway

☐ Panama

☐ Paraguay

☐ Portugal

☐ Qatar

☐ Saudi Arabia

☐ Scotland

☐ Senegal

☐ South Africa

☐ South Korea

☐ Spain

☐ Switzerland

☐ Tunisia

☐ United States

☐ Uruguay

☐ Uzbekistan

World Cup 2026 Group Edition

☐ Group A

☐ Group B

☐ Group C

☐ Group D

☐ Group E

☐ Group F

☐ Group G

☐ Group H

☐ Group I

☐ Group J

☐ Group K

☐ Group L

English Football Edition

- ☐ Arsenal F.C.
- ☐ Aston Villa F.C.
- ☐ Chelsea F.C.
- ☐ Everton F.C.
- ☐ Fulham F.C.
- ☐ Liverpool F.C.
- ☐ Manchester City
- ☐ Manchester United
- ☐ Newcastle United F.C.
- ☐ Tottenham Hotspur
- ☐ West Ham United
- ☐ Wrexham A.F.C.

NBA Edition

- ☐ Atlanta Hawks
- ☐ Boston Celtics
- ☐ Brooklyn Nets
- ☐ Charlotte Hornets
- ☐ Chicago Bulls
- ☐ Cleveland Cavaliers
- ☐ Dallas Mavericks
- ☐ Denver Nuggets
- ☐ Detroit Pistons
- ☐ Golden State Warriors
- ☐ Houston Rockets
- ☐ Indiana Pacers
- ☐ LA Clippers
- ☐ Los Angeles Lakers
- ☐ Memphis Grizzlies
- ☐ Miami Heat
- ☐ Milwaukee Bucks
- ☐ Minnesota Timberwolves
- ☐ New Orleans Pelicans
- ☐ New York Knicks
- ☐ Oklahoma City Thunder
- ☐ Orlando Magic
- ☐ Philadelphia 76ers
- ☐ Phoenix Suns
- ☐ Portland Trail Blazers
- ☐ Sacramento Kings
- ☐ San Antonio Spurs
- ☐ Toronto Raptors
- ☐ Utah Jazz
- ☐ Washington Wizards

About the Author

Jake is a 13-year-old sports fan who loves football, American football, and basketball. He plays soccer as a goalie and dreams of one day playing for West Ham United and helping teach kids to love the game. His passion for sports runs in the family - his dad was a professional baseball player, and his stepdad sparked his love for West Ham. Through the Fun Fan Facts series, he shares the fun and excitement of sports with fans everywhere.

www.ingramcontent.com/pod-product-compliance
Lightning Source LLC
Chambersburg PA
CBHW050040040726
47599CB00015B/1764